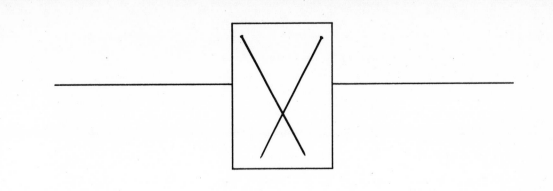

KNITTING

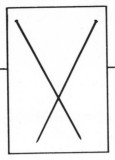

BY MARY WALKER PHILLIPS

KNITTING

*Illustrated with
photographs and drawings*

*Franklin Watts
New York/London/1977*

Photographs courtesy of:

The United Nations: pp. 3 and 6
Cotton Incorporated: p. 8
Fred Albert: all other photographs

Diagrams by Vantage Art, Inc.

Library of Congress Cataloging in Publication Data

Phillips, Mary Walker.
   Knitting.

   Bibliography: p.
   Includes index.
   SUMMARY: An introduction to knitting includ-
ing discussions of yarn, equipment, stitches, and
complete directions for several projects.
     1. Knitting—Juvenile literature.   [1. Knitting.
2. Handicraft]   I. Title.
TT820.P445   746.4'32   76–41717
ISBN 0–531–00837–1

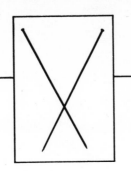

CONTENTS

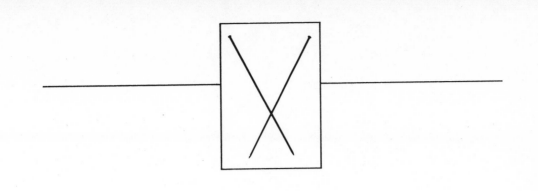

KNITTING

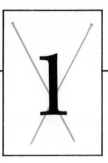

A HISTORY
OF KNITTING

Knitting is a way of making a fabric from one thread using two needles. People have been making clothes, rugs, and bedspreads in this way for hundreds of years. Some knitted garments were found in Egypt that had been made about 1,700 years ago. A kind of knitting was also being done in ancient Peru at about the same time.

Knitting was probably brought to Europe by Arab traders. By the time of the Middle Ages, people in European countries wore many clothes knitted from wool and silk. These included stockings, hats, shirts, gloves, and even coats. Some of them were beautifully decorated and embroidered. Rugs and carpets were also knitted.

The knitting craftsmen who made these things in Paris, France, were proud of their work, and they joined together in a Knitters' Guild. Later, other countries had knitters' guilds too. These groups of craftsmen set standards for good work. They controlled the sale of knitted goods and saw that fair prices were paid for them. They also trained young men to become knitters.

The training took six years. The young man, who was called an apprentice, spent three years learning the basics of knitting. Then he went abroad to study knitting in other countries. When he had finished his training, he had to show examples of his work to the master craftsmen before he could be admitted to the guild. He had to knit a woolen shirt, a beret, and a pair of woolen socks with decorations up the side called clocks. He also had to knit a carpet with a very complicated design. All these samples had to be made in thirteen weeks. When he had passed the examination, the knitter was allowed to wear a special hat, made of felted knitting, for his first year in the guild.

The knitters of the guilds were all men, but as knitting spread and was done at home, more and more women learned to knit. Knitting schools were started in England to train children for the knitting trade. When an English minister, the Reverend William Lee, invented a machine for knitting stockings, framework knitting (as it was called) became an important trade. But people still went on knitting by hand, and for a long time hand-knitting was a flourishing trade too.

In colonial times, both boys and girls learned to knit when they were very small. Besides clothing, many American women knitted rugs, bedspreads, and tablecloths for their homes. The work was often very delicate, using fine cotton or linen thread. Sometimes a knitter would make a sampler showing all the different stitches and patterns. The patterns had names, such as diamond, star, lace diadem, bramble, leaf, shell, and popcorn, just as embroidery stitches have names. You can see knitting samplers in some museums.

The Hopi Indians learned to knit from the Spanish explorers. The men and boys of the tribe were the knitters. They made the leggings worn by the men at ceremonies. These leggings were knitted of black, white, and indigo blue yarn.

In Sololá, Guatemala, the men are the knitters. They make beautiful bags in designs that have been used for more than a hundred years. They knit as they sit outside their stores or their homes.

Some lovely work comes from the Cuzco area of the Peruvian Andes, where knitting has been a craft for many hundreds of years. You'll remember that some of the very earliest examples of knitting were found in Peru. There are caps in complicated designs that use rich, glowing colors. All the caps have earflaps for protection against the cutting mountain winds. The people of this area also knit animals and flowers, as well as sweaters and poncho-type garments.

Bolivian Indian woman knitting.
Notice the girl's knitted sweater.

Today knitting is popular again in the United States. It is easy to learn, as you will see from this book, and there are so many different things you can make, quickly and simply. You can carry your work around with you, and your material—the yarn and the needles—don't cost much. With very little trouble you can have something good-looking that you have made yourself.

YARNS

Today there are many different kinds of yarns. The yarn you pick will depend, of course, on what you have decided to make. You can choose yarns that come from animal fibers or from plants, or even yarns that do not come from any growing thing at all but are made chemically in factories.

ANIMAL FIBERS

Wool comes from sheep. At the beginning of the summer, the soft, curly hair, or fleece, of the sheep is cut off. This makes the animal more comfortable in the heat, and by the time the weather turns cold again, its fleece will have grown back. The fleece is cleaned and combed, and then the small pieces are spun and twisted into one long thread of yarn. Usually the spinning is done by machine, but in the old days it was done by hand, using a spinning wheel.

Wool is soft and light in weight, but it is warm in winter and keeps its shape well. Wool yarn comes in many thicknesses.

Other animals whose coats are used to make yarn are goats, rabbits, camels, alpacas, llamas, and vicuñas.

The South American llama is
one source of wool for knitting.

Mohair comes from Angora goats. It too is soft, light, and warm, but it is fluffier than wool. The hair of a special kind of goat, found only in Tibet and in the northwestern provinces of China, is used for a very soft, expensive yarn called cashmere.

Angora, which is another soft, fluffy yarn that is sometimes used in making baby clothes, comes from the Angora rabbit.

The coat of the alpaca, an animal that is found mainly in the South American Andes, is the source of alpaca yarn. This tough, fine yarn has been used for centuries by the South Americans in both knitting and weaving. The llama, from the same region, has a wool that is inferior to alpaca wool. Vicuñas too are found in South America. Before the arrival of the conquistadores in the sixteenth century, only Inca chiefs and Indians of high rank were allowed to wear clothes made from its soft, silky hair.

Silk is an animal fiber too, but it doesn't come from an animal's coat. It is a fiber made by silkworms, which are a kind of caterpillar. They make it for their cocoons, when they are changing into moths. The finest silk comes from silkworms fed on mulberry leaves. China and Japan produce the most silk, but it is also made in India, Italy, and France. It is a very fine but strong fiber and when it is knitted, it makes a beautiful, lightweight, rich-looking fabric.

PLANT FIBERS

The most common plant fibers are cotton and linen. Cotton grows in several parts of the United States and also in other parts of the world. Whole fields are sown with cotton. After the plants have grown and flowered, the flower falls off and the cotton fibers grow inside a protective covering, called a boll. The cotton is harvested in the fall and is sent to textile mills, where it is cleaned and then spun into thread. Cotton is hard-wearing and absorbs moisture well.

Linen comes from the flax plant, but it comes from the stem of the plant, not from the seed as cotton does. The ancient Egyptians used linen to make clothes, and tomb paintings have been found that show just how the linen was spun and woven in Egypt 4,000 years ago. In

These cotton plants are ready for harvest.
They will be cleaned and spun into thread.

the past it was used for robes worn on special occasions by kings and priests. Today fine handkerchiefs, tablecloths, and sometimes sheets are woven from it.

MAN-MADE FIBERS

These fibers, which are also called synthetic fibers, are made chemically. They include rayon, nylon, polyester, and acrylic. Sometimes they are used alone, but they are also combined with natural fibers. Synthetic fibers are quick-drying and hard-wearing, but they are not as warm or as absorbent as wool.

OTHER THINGS
YOU SHOULD KNOW
ABOUT YARN

Not only do yarns come from different sources, they are also made in different thicknesses and textures and, of course, dyed in many different colors.

Some yarn is very fine and smooth and can be used for baby clothes. Thick, strong yarn can be knitted into bulky sweaters and blankets. Some yarn has bumps in it, called slub, which gives an interesting bumpy texture to the knitting.

Dyeing

Fiber is sometimes dyed before it is spun, but more often this is done after spinning. Besides solid colors, you can buy yarn called ombré, which has several shades of the same color, or even contrasting colors, at intervals along the yarn thread. Some yarn has a mixture of colors spun together, so that it looks like tweed.

Yarn is dyed in lots, or batches, and no two lots are exactly the same color, though they come pretty close. Each lot is given a special number, and when it is sold, the lot number is printed on the wrapper.

Make sure that all the yarn you buy for a project comes from the same dye lot.

Buying Yarn

You buy yarn in skeins or balls, each with a paper around it. Usually it is ready to use, but if not, you will have to wind it into a ball yourself. Wind the ball loosely, so that you don't stretch the yarn. The easiest way is to wind the yarn over at least two fingers as well as the ball. Keep slipping the yarn off your fingers onto the ball. Turn the ball each time you slip the yarn off, so that you have a nice round ball.

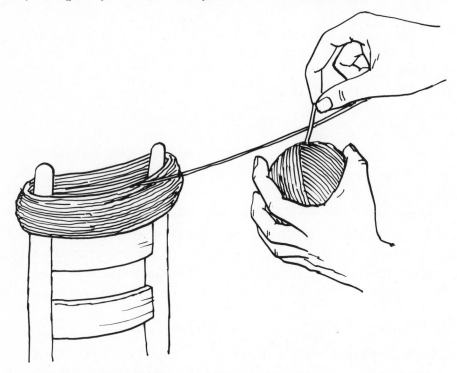

Look carefully at the wrapper around the yarn. It will tell you:

type of yarn (the fiber it is made from)
amount of yarn (in ounces)
color name and dye lot number
thickness
washing instructions

All this is important information that you need to make your knitting turn out the way it should. Your directions will tell you the type of yarn to buy, the thickness you need, and the amount you need for the project. The color is up to you.

The projects in the second half of this book tell you what type of yarn to use. You will see such terms as rug yarn and knitting worsted. Here is a list of the different thicknesses you are likely to meet as you do more knitting:

baby yarn	wool or synthetic	very thin yarn, used for baby clothes (not used for any projects in this book)
sport yarn (includes Shetland)	wool or synthetic	thin yarn, used for socks, light sweaters, some children's clothes, scarves
worsted	wool or synthetic	medium thick yarn, used for sweaters, hats, blankets, coat hanger covers, toys
Nantuck	synthetic	different thicknesses of yarn, suitable for various projects
rug yarn	mixture of rayon and cotton	very heavy, thick yarn, used for pot holders, slippers, rugs, coat hanger covers, bags
cotton yarn	cotton	washcloths, place mats
carpet warp	cotton	used double for place mats, bags
macramé cord	cotton or synthetic	medium thick cord, used for bags

NEEDLES AND
OTHER EQUIPMENT

Most knitting needles are made of plastic, aluminum, steel, or wood. There are three basic kinds—single-pointed, double-pointed, and circular.

When learning to knit, most people use two single-pointed needles. The stitches are moved from one needle to the other as they are knitted.

As you grow more comfortable with knitting, you may prefer to use a circular needle, which has points at each end and a coiled nylon section in the middle. This type of needle can be used for any pattern meant for two single-pointed needles. I like a circular needle best and I prefer a plastic one. I like it because all the weight of the knitting is in my lap, instead of being held up by my arms as it would be on two needles. Also, there is nothing to catch on the arms of my chair, as there is with two needles.

Double-pointed needles are used for knitting socks and anything else that has to be knitted like a tube, without seams.

Needles come in different lengths and thicknesses. Single-pointed needles are sold in pairs, and you can buy them in two lengths—short (10 inches) and long (14 inches). Double-pointed needles are sold in sets of four, or sometimes five, and generally they are 7 inches long; 10-inch double-pointed needles are also available.

Circular needles come in different lengths and in all thicknesses.

The thickness of a needle is shown by its size number. In the United States, the thinnest needle is size 0, and the sizes go up to the fat size 15. It is the other way around in England and Canada, where the fattest needle is size 0 and the thinnest has a high number.

The thinnest needles are used with thin yarn to make very delicate, fine stitches. The fatter the needle and the thicker the yarn, the bigger and looser the stitch. You can buy a needle gauge to measure your needles, if the size is not marked on them. This is a piece of plastic or metal that has a number of holes in it, each hole a different needle size. You put your needle into each hole until you find the one that it fits exactly. The gauge is often marked off in inches on one side, so that you can measure the length of your knitting.

MAKING YOUR OWN NEEDLES

You can make your own wooden needles. To make three pairs you will need:

> 2 wooden dowels (shaped like cylinders) from the hardware store, 36 inches long and the thickness of the needle you need (take your needle gauge to the store with you)
> 6 corks or 6 beads with holes almost wide enough to hold the dowel
> a pencil sharpener
> sandpaper
> glue
> wood stain if you want to color your needles

Cut each dowel into three pieces, each 12 inches long. Use the pencil sharpener to put a point on one end of each dowel. Make sure the point is not too sharp, or you will hurt your fingers and split the yarn. Then sharpen the other end of the needle a little, until it will fit in the hole in the bead or can be pushed into the cork. Now smooth the dowels carefully with the sandpaper, so that there are no rough places to catch the yarn. Follow the directions on the packet of wood stain if you are staining the needles. Put a little glue on the dowel tip and fix it in the bead or the cork.

OTHER THINGS
YOU WILL NEED
IN YOUR WORKBASKET

Crochet hooks. These are straight needles with a hook at one end. You will need them for picking up dropped stitches (see page 34) and perhaps for putting an edging on your knitting.

A needle gauge.

Needle-point protectors, made either of rubber (purchased) or of cork (made by you).

"T" pins for blocking your finished work (see pages 37–38).

Rulers (6-inch and 12-inch) and a measuring tape.

Tapestry needles in two or more sizes, for sewing in loose ends of yarn and for sewing knitted pieces together. These needles are easy to thread and have dull points.

Scissors (I prefer blunt to sharp).

Emery boards for smoothing rough spots on your needles or your fingernails, so that the yarn is not caught on them.

Ring markers for identifying different sections in your knitting.

STORING YOUR
KNITTING EQUIPMENT

When you use cotton yarn on spools you must be careful that the yarn is always pulled out sideways. If you pull it straight up, the yarn will be given an extra twist. You can easily make a special box for holding spools of yarn. You will need:

a shoebox

a dowel at least 2 inches longer than the box and slightly thinner
than the holes in the spools (so they can be threaded on it)

two corks

glue

a pencil sharpener

scissors with sharp points

Cut a hole in the middle of each end of the shoebox that is large enough
for the dowel to go through. Be careful to put the holes exactly opposite
each other. Sharpen each end of the dowel with the pencil sharpener
and glue a cork on one end only. Push the other end of the dowel from
the outside through the hole in the shoebox. Slip the spools onto the
dowel and then push the point of the dowel through the hole in the
other end of the box. The second cork can then be put on the end, but
this one must not be glued as you will want to take it off whenever you
need to add or take away a spool. You can decorate the box however
you like.

STORING NEEDLES

You will probably want to keep your needles separate from your yarn
when you are not using them. You could store your needles in another
shoebox, a plastic box from the dime store, a glass jar, a pottery jug,
or a pretty basket.

YOUR WORKBASKET

This doesn't have to be a basket, though there are many inexpensive
ones to be found in stores. You can use a shopping bag or a cloth bag you
have made yourself or a box that is large enough to hold everything
you need. However you store all the things you use in knitting, make
sure that you keep them tidy and can find them whenever you want

them. Always finish a row before you put your knitting away and don't poke the needles through the knitting or you will make holes in it. If you put the needles side by side, you can wrap the yarn around them two or three times. Keep light-colored knitting clean by wrapping it in a cloth or a large handkerchief.

BEGINNING TO KNIT

In knitting, you hold the needle with stitches on it in your left hand. As you knit each stitch, it is put onto the right-hand needle. When all the stitches have been knitted from the left-hand needle to the right-hand one, you have knitted a row.

There are two ways you can hold the yarn in knitting—with your left hand or with your right. The first is called the "German" or "Continental" method, and the second is known as the "English" method. You should probably try both and choose whichever one you find most comfortable. The "Continental" method is especially good for people who are left-handed.

CASTING ON

There are several ways to cast on. Here is one of the easiest and the best. Measure off enough yarn for the stitches you need. If you are using heavy yarn, you should allow about 1 inch for each stitch. With lighter-weight yarn, you only need about ½ inch to each stitch. Give yourself a little extra to be safe; you can always use any leftover yarn for sewing up your work later.

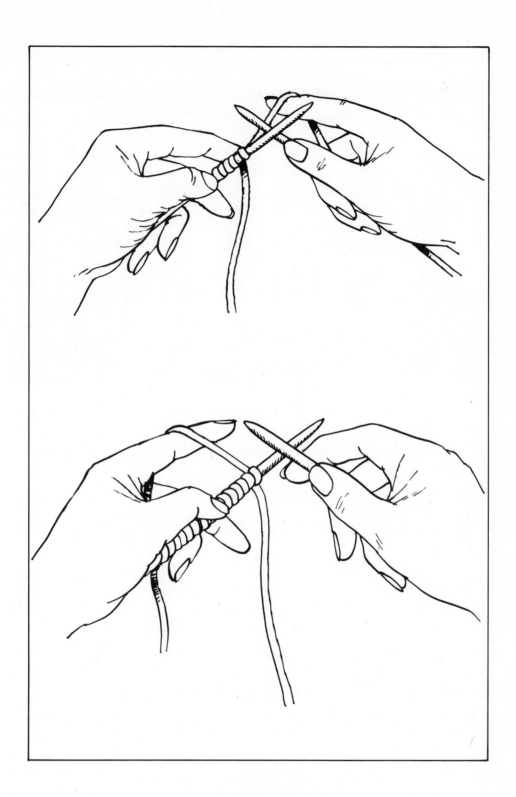

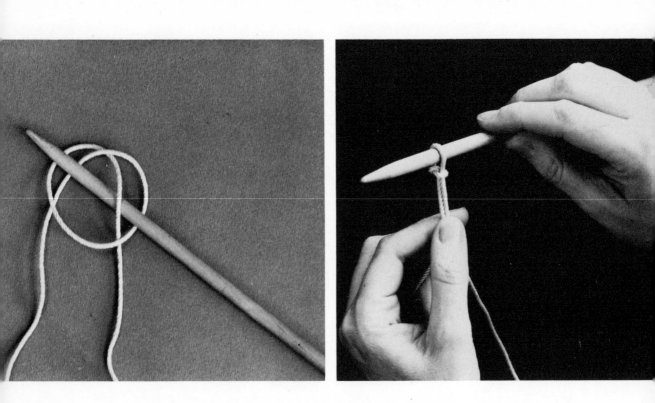

1. Put the needle through the yarn to make a slipknot.
2. Pull the ends of the yarn tight against the needle.
3. Hold the needle in your right hand. Spread your left hand as the photograph shows. Put your thumb under the free end of the yarn. The yarn that is joined to the ball goes over your left forefinger. Hold both strands of yarn under the last three fingers of your left hand.
4. Turn your hand so that your fingers are closer together.
5. Put the needle through the loop on your thumb and pick up the thread on your forefinger with the needle point.
6. Pull the thread through so that it makes a stitch on the needle. Tighten the free end by pulling against it with your thumb. At the same time, you will be looping the free end around your thumb again, so that you will be ready to make the next new stitch.

Repeat these six steps until you have enough stitches. Be careful not to pull the stitches too tight. You want them to slide easily along the needle.

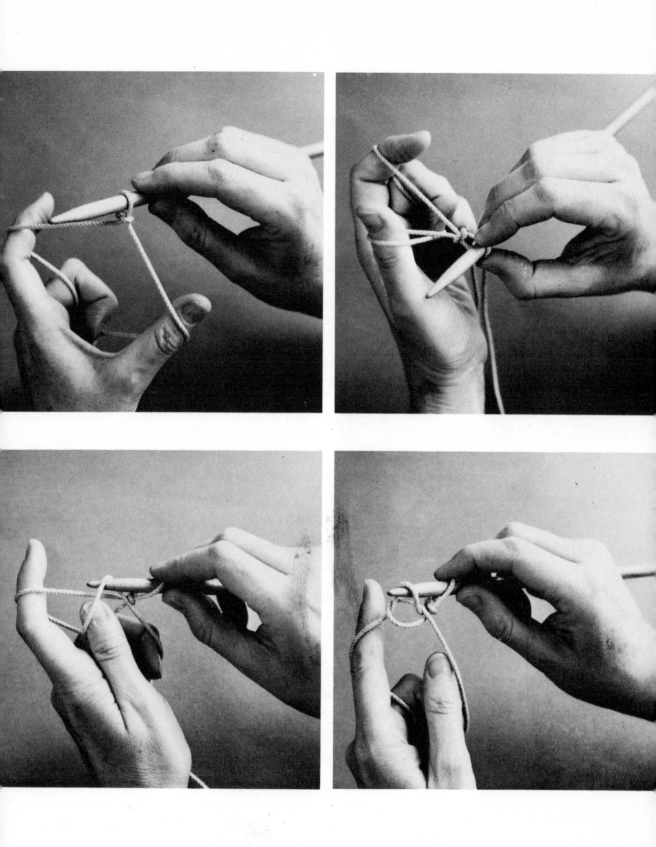

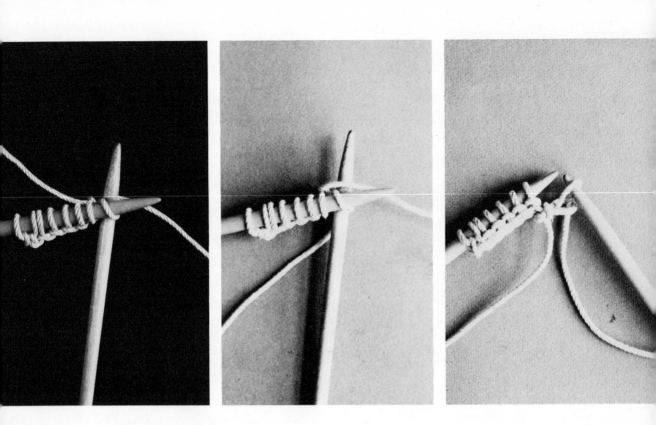

HOW TO KNIT

The "knit" stitch is a basic stitch. It is used alone and it is also used as part of many patterns. This is how you do it. Hold the needle with stitches on it in your left hand and the empty needle in your right.

1. Put the point of the right-hand needle through the first stitch on the left-hand needle from front to back, so that the right-hand point is behind the left-hand point.
2. Wrap the yarn between the two needles, across the loop.
3. Bring the right-hand needle point back to the front, pulling the yarn with it through the old stitch to make a new one.
4. Pull the old stitch off the left-hand needle. Now your new stitch is on the right-hand needle.

Follow these four steps for each of the stitches on your left-hand needle until you have finished the row.

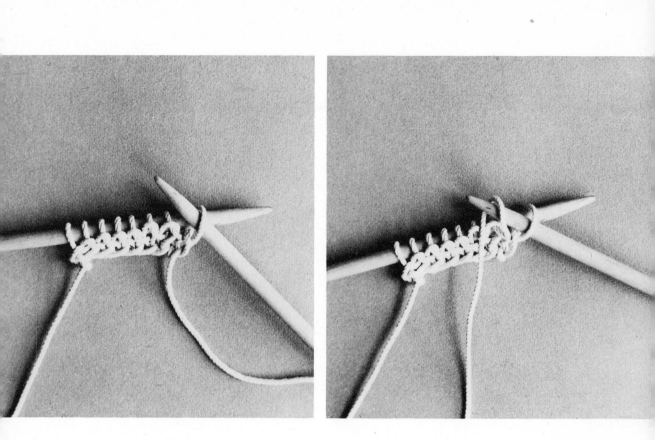

HOW TO PURL

This is an easy basic stitch too. Purl is often used with knit to make other stitches such as the stockinette stitch and the rib stitch. To knit a purl stitch, hold the needle with stitches in your left hand and bring the yarn to the front. Hold the empty needle in your right hand.

1. Put the point of the right-hand needle through the first stitch, from back to front (the opposite of knit), so that the right-hand point is in front of the left-hand point.

2. Wrap the yarn around the right-hand needle.

3. Bring the right-hand needle point under the left-hand one, pulling the yarn with it to make a new stitch.

4. Pull the old stitch off the left-hand needle. The new stitch is on the right-hand needle.

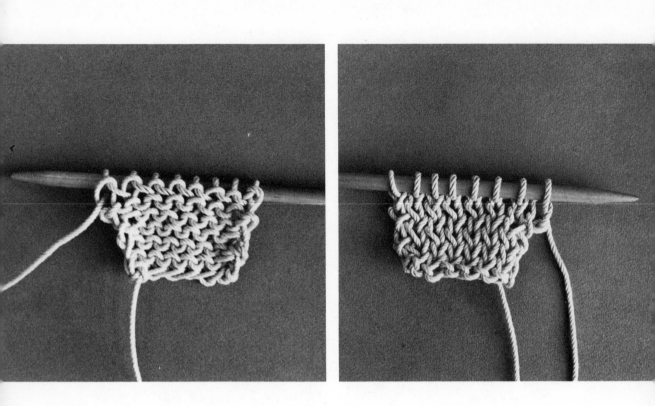

TWO SIMPLE STITCHES

Here are two very easy stitches that you will use a lot.

Garter Stitch

Knit every row. When the outside of the work is toward you, you will see that the row you are knitting is smooth, but that the last row you knitted made a ridge. There is one ridge for every two rows.

Stockinette Stitch

Knit one row. Purl one row. Repeat these rows. The outside of your work will be smooth, and the inside will have ridges, one for every row. You always knit when the outside is facing you and purl when the inside is facing you. The photographs show the smooth outside (all knit stitches) and the ridges inside (all purl stitches).

[24]

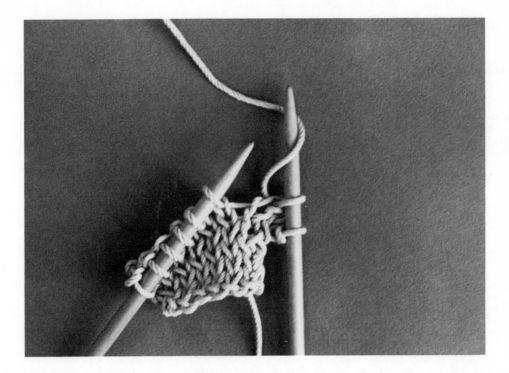

SHAPING

Sometimes you will want your knitting to get wider or narrower. To
shape it, you will have to increase or decrease the number of stitches on
your needle.

Increasing

There are two ways of doing this. One is called "yarn over." The other
is knitting twice in the same stitch. Your directions will tell you which
one to use.

Yarn Over

This is a way of increasing, but you can also use "yarn over" to make
a hole as part of a pattern. You bring the yarn to the front of your
knitting and wrap it over the right-hand needle before knitting the
next stitch.

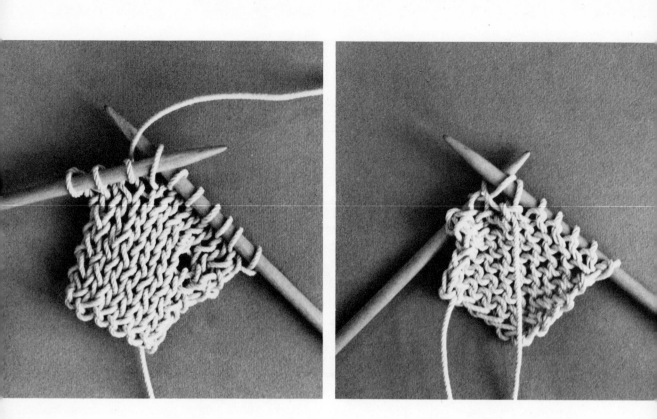

On the next row, knit or purl (depending, of course, on the pattern you are doing) into the *back* of the yarn-over stitch if you don't want a hole. If you *do* want a hole as part of your pattern, then knit or purl into the front.

Knitting Twice
in the Same Stitch

This way of increasing doesn't make a hole. There are two steps:

1. Knit the stitch where you are making the increase in the usual way, but *don't* pull it off the left-hand needle.

2. Knit the same stitch again, but this time put your needle into the back of the stitch to knit it. Slip the old stitch off the left-hand needle.

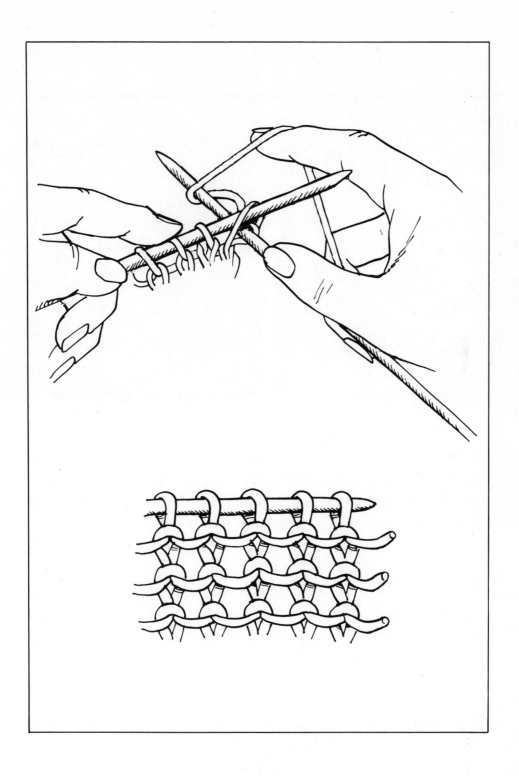

Decreasing

There are two ways of doing this too, either by knitting two stitches together or by passing the slipped stitch over. Your directions will tell you which one to use.

Knitting Two
Stitches Together

Knit two stitches together as if they are one stitch. This gives a left to right slant to the decrease. You can see this in the photograph.

Passing the
Slipped Stitch Over

To get a right to left slant, use this method. Put your needle into the stitch on the left-hand needle as though you were going to purl it, and

slip it onto the right-hand needle. Knit the next stitch in the usual way. Then, using the point of the left-hand needle, pass the slipped stitch over the one you have just knitted.

CASTING OFF

To finish off your knitting, knit the first two stitches of the row onto the right-hand needle.

1. Put the left-hand needle point through the first stitch you knitted and slip it over the second.
2. Knit another stitch onto the right-hand needle.

Repeat these two steps until you have only one stitch left. Cut the yarn at least 3 inches from the knitting. Pull the end of the yarn through the last stitch and pull it tight.

KNITTING TERMS

Before you begin to read knitting directions, you will have to learn the short forms that knitters use. These are very easy. Here is a list of the ones used in this book.

k	knit (see page 22)
p	purl (see page 23)
st, sts	stitch, stitches
yo	yarn over (see page 25), used for increasing and for decoration
tog	knit stitches together (see page 28), to make a left to right slant (used for decreasing)
sl	slip a stitch, as if to purl, from the left-hand needle to the right-hand needle without knitting
psso	pass the slipped stitch over the following stitch (see page 28) to make a right to left slant (used for decreasing)
inc	increase
dec	decrease
*	shows that the directions following the * are to be repeated
( )	knitting directions that are inside parentheses should be repeated the number of times given in the directions that follow the parentheses; for example, (k 2 p 2) twice.

STITCHES AND PATTERNS THAT ARE USED IN THE PROJECTS

GARTER STITCH AND STOCKINETTE STITCH

In the garter stitch, you knit every row (see page 24). In the stockinette stitch, you knit one row and purl the next row (see page 24).

RIB STITCH

Here knit and purl are used in turn, usually on an even number of stitches. This makes a pattern of ribs, or ridges, that go up and down the knitting. The most common rib stitch is k 1 p 1 across each row. Remember to take the yarn to the back for knit stitches and to the front for purl. If you don't do this, you will find yourself with a lot of yarn-overs. You always do knit stitches on top of knit stitches in rib, and purl stitches on top of purl. Some patterns are in k 2 p 2 rib or even k 4 p 4. Of course this gives a much wider rib.

SEED STITCH

This can be done on an odd or even number of stitches.

      Odd number: * K 1, p 1, repeat from * across to last stitch, k 1.
                    Repeat every row.
      Even number: Row 1: * K 1, p 1, repeat from * across row.
                    Row 2: * P 1, k 1, repeat from * across row.

This stitch is the opposite of rib because you purl every stitch that was knit in the row before and knit every purl stitch.

RICE STITCH

This must be done on an even number of stitches.

      Row 1: K across row (front of knitting).
      Row 2: * K 1, p 1, repeat from * across row.

PURSE STITCH

This must be done on an even number of stitches.

      * Yo p 2 tog, repeat from * across row. All rows are the same. When you actually use this stitch, you will need one or two edge stitches at either end of the row before you start the pattern, because it is very hard to start a row with yo, and it makes a ragged edge.

MODIFIED
LACE STITCH

You will need a number of stitches that divides by 2 for this pattern. Like the purse stitch, this lacy pattern needs edge stitches, but they aren't included in the directions for the pattern itself.

      Row 1: * Yo k 2 tog, repeat from * across row.
      Row 2: K across row.

LEAF PATTERN

You will need a number of stitches that divides by 6 for this pattern. You will also need edge stitches, but they aren't included in the directions for the pattern itself.

    Row 1: * Yo, k 3 tog, yo, k 3, repeat from * across row.

    Rows 2 and 4: P across row.

    Row 3: * K 3, yo, k 3 tog, yo, repeat from * across row.

HELPFUL HINTS

MISTAKES ANYONE CAN MAKE
AND HOW TO PUT THEM RIGHT

Don't worry if you make mistakes. Even experienced knitters sometimes do things like dropping stitches or not counting their stitches carefully. Mistakes can nearly always be corrected, even if you have to rip back some of what you have done and do it over.

Dropped Stitches

If you do drop a stitch, pick it up and put it back on the needle as quickly as possible. Otherwise the finished work will have a hole in it. To pick up a knit stitch, put the crochet hook through the loop from the front of the knitting, pick up the strand of yarn behind it, and pull it through. With a dropped purl stitch, start from the back of the knitting. Put the crochet hook through the loop of the dropped stitch and pull the strand through to the back.

Ripped Stitches

Sometimes, if you have made a bad mistake, or if you have knitted more than the directions told you to, you will have to rip back a few rows.

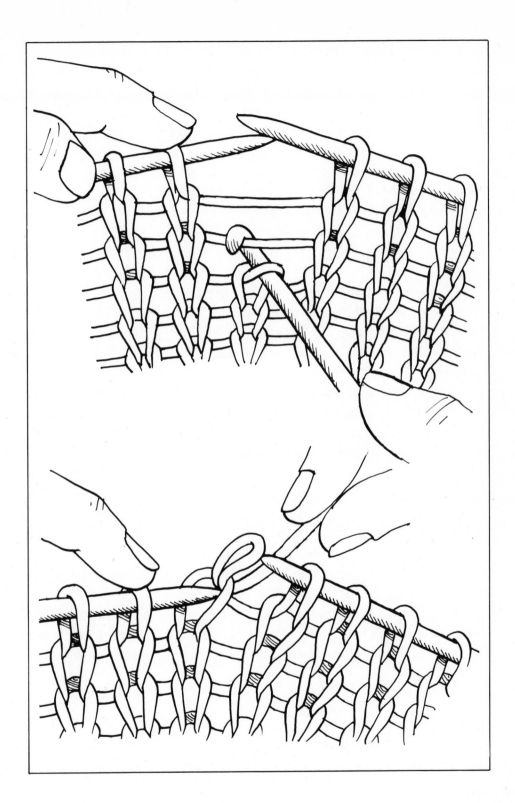

To do this, you will have to take your work off the needles. Then pull the yarn strand slowly, until you have ripped the necessary number of rows. When you have ripped back enough, be very careful to put the stitches back on the needles the right way. Check the knit and purl photographs on pages 22–23 if you aren't sure which is the right way.

OTHER THINGS YOU SHOULD KNOW ABOUT

Gauge

The gauge is the number of stitches across a 1-inch width of knitting. When you come to the projects on page 43, you will see that the directions for each one include the gauge. You should always check your gauge before you start a project to make sure that the work ends up the right size.

Here's how to check your gauge. Use the yarn described in the directions and the needles of the suggested size and knit a sample about 4 inches square. (Though you are only going to measure 2 inches, the bigger size gives a better sample of the way you are knitting.) If the directions tell you to block the finished piece (blocking is described on page 37), then block your sample before you measure it. Measure a 2-inch square of your sample and count the number of stitches across its width. Then divide by 2. If you have too many stitches in your 2-inch section for the gauge given, then your knitting is too tight and you should try a size bigger needle. If you have too few stitches, try a size smaller needle.

Don't worry too much about the gauge for the projects in this book, since none of them have to fit exactly. But in the future, when you are making clothes where size is important, watch your gauge carefully.

Joining Yarn

If you have to join in a new piece of yarn, do it at the beginning of a row. Tie the old end to the new end with a square knot, leaving a few

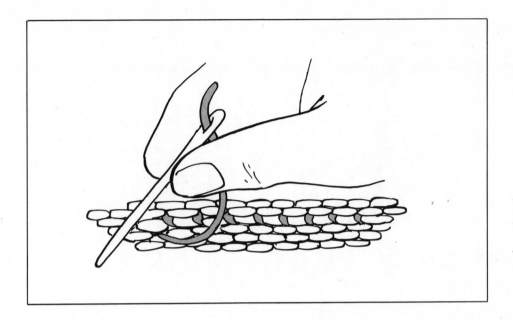

inches at each end. When you have finished your work, untie half of the square knot. Use a tapestry needle to weave each end into the work in opposite directions along the edge.

Finishing Your Work

This is a very important part of any knitting project. First, weave in the ends of any joins, as described above. Then check to see if your directions tell you to block your work.

Blocking

Blocking is a method used to form the knitting into its final shape, to make sure it is the right size and that it is smooth and flat. If you are going to do a lot of knitting, you might want to make yourself a special blocking board out of Celotex or cork (which you can buy in most hobby shops). Otherwise you can use any surface that you can put pins into. Your mother might let you use her ironing board.

For blocking you will need:

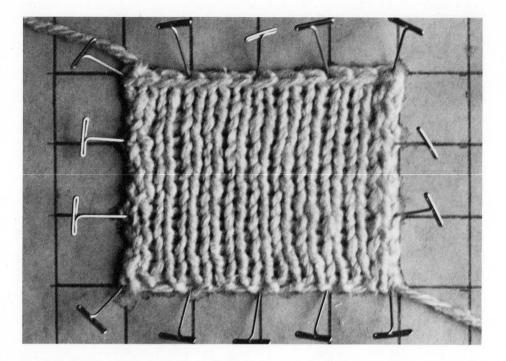

a blocking board or flat surface

a piece of brown paper ruled into 1-inch squares

masking tape

a bowl of warm water (add a little fabric softener for wool and synthetic yarns because this cuts down the static electricity)

a towel

some "T" pins (you can get these from a hobby shop or a shop that sells sewing supplies)

Tape the brown paper to the flat surface. Put the knitting in the water just long enough to dampen it; don't soak it. Take it out and roll it in the towel to soak up the extra moisture. Spread your work out carefully on the paper so that it fits exactly the measurements given in the directions, stretching it a little if you have to. Then pin it in place and let it dry.

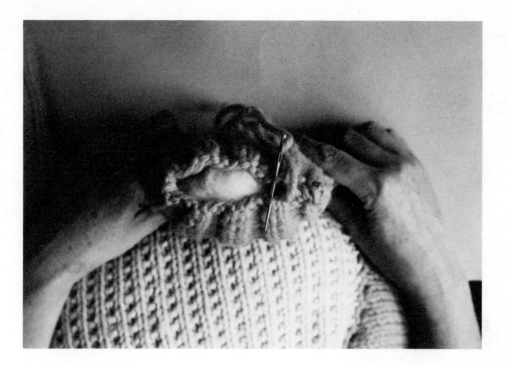

Sewing Up

If your project needs sewing, this should be done after the blocking. Pin the pieces together, making sure that they match exactly. Then, using a tapestry needle threaded with the yarn you used to knit with, sew the pieces together with an overcast stitch. Don't pull the stitches too tight or the seam will be bumpy.

Fringes, Tassels, Braids, and Chains

You can trim scarves, hats, stoles, bags, and blankets with fringes, tassels, or braids. They are easy to make and they look cheerful.

Fringes
First, decide whether you want your fringe to be thick (as in the quex-quemitl on page 55) or spaced out (as in the blanket on page 62). Then figure out how many units of fringe you need. Each unit of fringe needs three 12-inch strands of yarn.

Loosely wrap your yarn lengthwise around a 12-inch ruler and cut it at both ends. Fold the strands in half. With the right side of your work facing you, take a crochet hook and pull the strands through to the back of the work. When you have pulled through enough to make a loop, put the ends through the loop and pull them gently. Put the crochet hook in the knot before you pull it tight. This is to make sure that the knot isn't too tight.

Tassels

Wind your yarn lengthwise around a 6-inch ruler, using as many strands as you need. Remember, if you want several tassels the same size, you

[40]

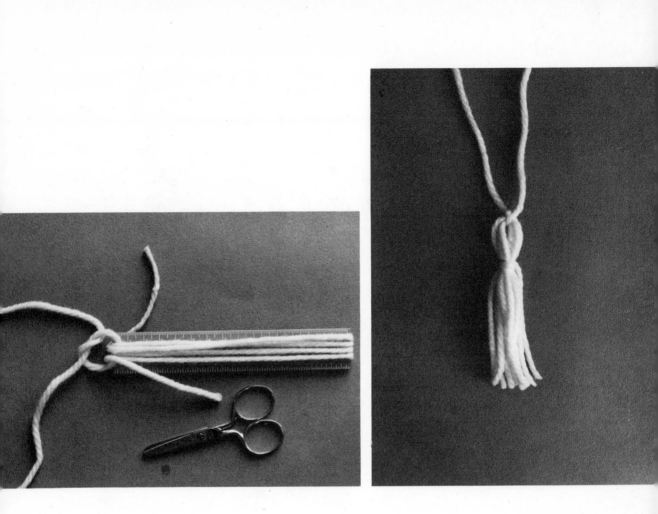

must use the same number of strands each time. Tie a piece of yarn at the top, around the strands (this can be used later to sew the tassel in place), and then cut the strands at the other end. Tie another piece of yarn around the strands 1 inch from the top.

Braids

Cut three strands of yarn three times the length you want your finished braid to be. Fold them in half and tie an overhand knot 3 inches from the looped end. Pull the strands down so that they lie straight and flat. Using two strands together, all through, take the two left-hand strands (marked 1 in the photograph) and cross them over the two cen-

[41]

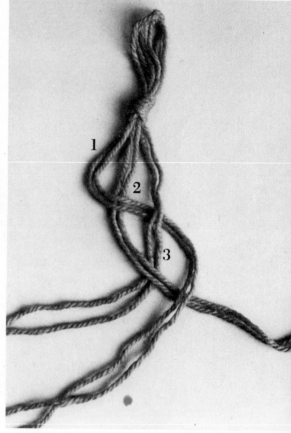

ter strands (marked 2). Then cross the two right-hand strands (marked 3) over 1, which have now become the center. Continue like this, crossing first the outside left strands over the center, then the right, and then the left again, until you have 3 inches of yarn left. Tie another overhand knot to finish off.

Chains

After casting off, keep the last stitch on the needle. Yarn over the needle and pull the yarn through the loop. Continue this until you have the required number of stitches. Leaving about 5 inches, cut the yarn and pull it carefully through the loop to close it.

8

PROJECTS

Try some of the simplest projects first, the ones that are done in garter stitch and have no shaping. This way you will get used to knitting and will find out the most comfortable way to hold your needles and yarn.

The colors suggested for the projects are only suggestions, and you can, of course, choose your own. The kind of yarn recommended, however, is important, and you should buy just what the directions tell you to, to be certain that the project will turn out right.

Soon, when you are comfortable with knitting, you will be able to make up your own patterns and designs, as well as knit projects from directions in other knitting books. At the end of this book you will find a list of other knitting books that may interest you.

Coat Hanger Cover

Materials: knitting worsted; ½ oz. each of 2 colors, to make two wooden hanger covers.

Needles: 1 pair No. 7 or English No. 6

Gauge: unnecessary here

Pattern: garter stitch

DIRECTIONS

Cast on 9 sts in first color. K 2 rows. Change to second color. K 2 rows. Repeat color scheme until you have 28 rows of the first color alternating with 27 rows of the second. Cast off. Leave 24 inches of yarn to sew the edges of the piece together.

To finish: Fold the piece in half lengthwise and sew each end. Insert the hook of the hanger in the center and continue sewing the cover on the hanger.

For fringe: Cut ten pieces of yarn 12 inches long. Fold the pieces in half. Put the middle of the yarn at the back of the hook, bring the ends on either side of the hook and then bring the yarn to the front of the hanger. Take the yarn under the hanger to the back, bring it to the front of the hook again, and tie in a square knot.

Variations

Use synthetic yarn if you prefer. You can also use ombré yarn. If you do, K 56 rows.

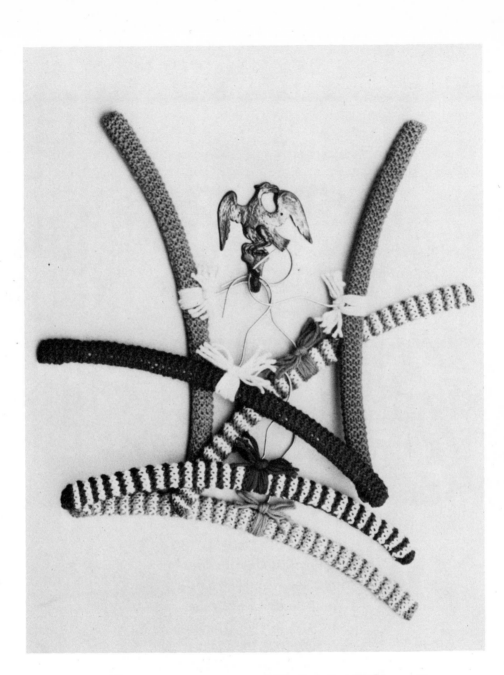

Coat Hanger Cover: *garter stitch. Bernhard Ulmann Co.,*
100% wool Knitting Worsted, in red and white,
green and white, turquoise and white, and solid colors.

Fat Cat's Delight
(Animal Blanket): *garter*
stitch. American Thread Co.,
Aunt Lydia's Heavy Rug
Yarn (cotton and rayon,
colorfast), Art. 235 in
No. 320 Burnt Orange and
No. 620 Hemlock, with
bells on the four corners.

Fat Cat's Delight (Animal Blanket)

Materials: rug yarn (cotton and rayon, colorfast; 70-yd. skein). 3 skeins each of 2 colors. If the blanket is for a cat, you can add 4 bells.

Needles: 1 pair No. 10 or English No. 3

Gauge: 3½ sts = 1 inch

Finished size: 18 inches square

Pattern: garter stitch

DIRECTIONS

Cast on 63 sts in first color. * K 16 rows. Change to second color. K 2 rows. Change to first color. K 2 rows. Repeat 2-row alternating color scheme twice more. Change to second color. K 16 rows. Change to first color. K 2 rows. Change to second color. K 2 rows. Repeat 2-row alternating color scheme twice more. Repeat from *. K 16 rows in first color. Cast off.

To finish: Work in ends of the yarn along the edges. If the blanket is for a cat, sew a bell on each corner.

Variations

You can choose the colors to match the room where the animal's basket will be, and you can vary the width of the stripes.

Striped Pillow

Materials: bulky Nantuck wool yarn (2-oz. skein). 1 skein each of 3 colors. Pillow form.

Needles: 1 pair No. 11 (no English size)

Gauge: 3 sts = 1 inch

Finished size: 13 inches square (2 pieces)

Pattern: stockinette stitch

DIRECTIONS

Cast on 39 sts in first color. * Row 1: K. Row 2: P. Change to second color. Repeat rows 1 and 2. Change to third color. Repeat rows 1 and 2. Repeat from * 7 more times. Work 1 more row in first color. Cast off. Repeat for second piece.

To finish: Block. Sew 3 sides together. Insert pillow form. Sew fourth side.

Variations

Stripes can be wider, or each color can be one third of the pillow. You can add a fringe or make a braid of the three colors (see page 41) and sew it around the edge.

*Striped Pillow: stockinette stitch.
Top photo: Columbia-Minerva Corp.,
Bulky Nantuck, Art. 2901, in No.
5434 Bermuda Blue, No. 5417 Winter
White, and No. 5442 Light Avocado.
Bottom photo: some variations.*

Belt with Bells

Materials: knitting worsted (1-oz. skein). 1 skein ombré. Four bells.

Needles: 1 pair No. 6 or English No. 7

Gauge: 4 sts = 1 inch

Finished size: 1½ inches by 38 inches

Pattern: seed stitch

DIRECTIONS

Cast on 7 sts. K 1, p 1 every row until all the yarn is knitted (or until the right waist size is reached). Leave enough yarn to cast off and to sew on the bells.

To finish: Sew bells on the four corners.

Variations

Knit this with cotton cord or metallic yarn.

Belt with Bells: seed stitch. Coats & Clark's Red Heart Ombré Knitting Worsted (100% wool), Art. E. 232 in No. 980 Ombré (orange to brown to yellow).

Pot Holders

Materials: rug yarn (cotton and rayon, colorfast; 70-yd. skein). 2 skeins each of 2 colors, or 4 skeins of 1 color if you are using only one. This will make four pot holders. Four 1-inch plastic curtain rings.

Needles: 1 pair No. 7 or English No. 6

Gauge: 4 sts = 1 inch in stripes; 3½ sts = 1 inch in solid color

Finished size: 8 inches by 7 inches

Pattern: garter stitch

DIRECTIONS

Solid color
Cast on 33 sts. K 58 rows. Cast off. Leave 6 inches of yarn to sew on the ring.

Alternating colors
Cast on 33 sts in first color. K 2 rows. Change to second color. K 2 rows. Repeat color scheme until 59 rows are completed, ending with first color. Cast off. Leave 6 inches of yarn to sew on the ring.

Pot Holders: garter stitch. American Thread Co., Aunt Lydia's Heavy Rug Yarn (cotton and rayon, colorfast), Art. 235 in No. 315 Tangerine and No. 740 Peacock.

Stripe

Cast on 33 sts in first color. K 10 rows. Change to second color. K 9 rows. Repeat color scheme twice more. K 1 row in first color. Cast off. Leave 6 inches of yarn to sew on the ring.

To finish: Sew the ring on a corner of the pot holder with yarn from casting off. Work beginning end of yarn into the edge of the pot holder and trim any yarn left over.

Variations

Make the squares larger and sew two together to make a hot pad. Knitted in knitting worsted and with larger needles, these make good squares for an afghan.

Knitted Quexquemitl

(pronounced *kish-ki-mal*)
Quexquemitls were worn by
women in ancient Mexico.

Materials: knitting worsted (2-oz. ball). 3 balls each of 3 colors.

Needles: 1 pair No. 8 or English No. 5

Gauge: 4½ sts = 1 inch

Finished size: 16 inches by 28 inches (2 pieces)

Pattern: seed stitch (* K 1, p 1, repeat from * across to last stitch, k 1.
Repeat every row)

DIRECTIONS

Leave at least 6 inches of yarn at the beginning and end of each color
change, to be used as part of the fringe. Cast on 73 sts in first color. Work
3 rows in seed stitch. Change to second color. Work 3 rows in seed stitch.
Change to third color. Work 3 rows in seed stitch. Repeat each color in
the same order 23 more times. Cast off. Repeat for second piece.

To finish: Block. Sew pieces together as in diagram. Cut as many pieces
of yarn 12 inches long of each color as necessary for fringe. Add 1 piece
of a contrasting color (first color with second, second with third, third
with first) to the ones you have, and make an overhand knot (see fringe
directions on page 39).

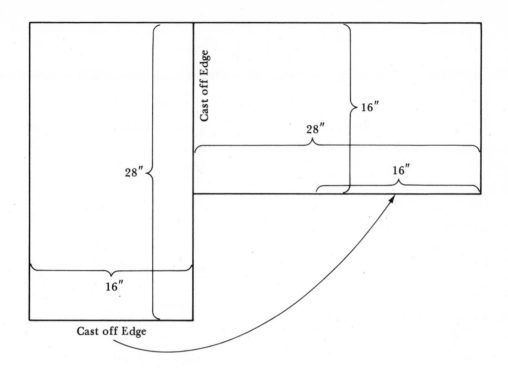

Variations

You can do the stripes with ombré wool alternating with a solid color. For a sarape-type garment, lay the two finished pieces side by side and sew them together, leaving an opening in the middle about 12 inches long for your head to go through. To make a stole, knit one piece the same width but twice as long.

Knitted Quexquemitl: *seed stitch. Bernhard Ulmann Co., Bear Brand 100% Wool Knitting Worsted, Art. 7150 in No. 418 Poison Green, No. 321 Hot Pink, and No. 56 Orange.*

Washcloth

Materials: cotton yarn (125-yd. ball). 2 balls each of 2 colors. This will make 2 washcloths.

Needles: 1 pair No. 7 or English No. 6

Gauge: 4½ sts = 1 inch

Finished size: 9½ inches square

Pattern: garter stitch on the bias

DIRECTIONS

Leave about 12 inches of yarn at the beginning. Cast on 2 sts in first color. Row 1: K 1, yo, k 1. Row 2: K 3. Row 3: K 1, yo, k 1, yo, k 1. Row 4: k 5. Continue inc in this way until you have 49 sts. Change to second color. K 18 rows. Change to first color. Begin dec as follows: Row A: k 2 tog, k to last 2 sts, k 2 tog. Row B: K across row. Repeat rows A and B until 3 sts remain. K 3 tog. K a chain of 24 sts (see page 42), and k a chain of 24 sts in the opposite corner.

To finish: Attach free end of chain to its beginning to make a loop for hanging.

Variations

Use colors alternately in stripes or use one solid color. This pattern can be knitted with heavier yarn to make pot holders.

Washcloth: *garter stitch on the bias.*
Lily Mills Co., Sugar and Cream
Cotton Yarn, Art. 930 in
No. 10 Yellow and No. 42 Pink.

Scarf

Materials: Nantuck synthetic sweater yarn (2-oz. skein). 1 skein each of 4 colors.

Needles: 1 pair No. 9 or English No. 4

Gauge: 9 sts = 2 inches

Finished size: 9 inches by 53 inches

Pattern: garter stitch on the bias

DIRECTIONS

Cast on 56 sts in first color. * Row 1: K 1, yo, k across row to last 2 sts, ending k 2 tog. Row 2: K across row. Repeat rows 1 and 2 until 16 rows are completed. Change to second color. Repeat rows 1 and 2 until 16 rows are completed. Change to third color. Repeat rows 1 and 2 until 16 rows are completed. Change to fourth color. Repeat rows 1 and 2 until 16 rows are completed. Repeat from * three more times. Change to first color. K 16 rows. Change to second color. K 16 rows. Cast off.

To finish: Add fringe if you like (see page 39).

Variations

You can use wider stripes or an ombré yarn for the whole scarf. If you fold the scarf in half and sew down from the fold for 9 inches, you have a head covering; you can wrap the rest of the scarf around your neck.

Scarf: garter stitch. Columbia-Minerva Corp., Nantuck Sweater and Afghan Yarn, Art. 2924 in No. 6303 Orange, No. 6326 Gold-3, No. 6307 Tangerine, and No. 6325 Gold-2.

Blanket

Materials: Win Knit synthetic knitting worsted (twin-pack, 2-oz. balls). 6 balls each of 3 colors.

Needles: 1 pair No. 8 or English No. 5

Gauge: 4½ sts = 1 inch

Finished size: 38 inches by 57 inches (1 square = 9½ inches square)

Pattern: garter stitch on the bias

DIRECTIONS

Cast on 2 sts in first color. Row 1: K 1, yo, k 1. Row 2 and all even rows: K (remember to k into backs of yo stitches). Row 3: K 1, yo, k 1, yo, k 1. Continue inc in this way on every odd number row until you have 41 sts. Change to second color. Continue in pattern for 2 rows. Begin alternating first and second colors every other row to 53 sts, ending in the second color (cut off the first color, leaving 10 inches). Continue in second color until you have 59 sts. Begin dec (odd number rows: K 1, sl 1, psso, k to last 2 sts, k 2 tog). Continue dec in this way every odd number row until you have 53 sts. Change to third color and continue in pattern for 2 rows. Begin alternating third and second color every other row until you have 41 sts, ending in third color (cut off the second color leaving 10 inches). Continue dec to 3 sts. K 3 tog. Leave 10 inches for finishing. Repeat the above pattern till you have 24 squares.

To finish: Block each square. Sew the squares together according to color, so that the first color comes at the center of each 4 squares sewn together. The finished blanket is 4 squares wide and 6 squares long. For fringe, see page 39.

Variations

To make a floor pillow, knit 8 squares in a heavier weight yarn, the front and the back in different colors.

Blanket: *garter stitch on the bias.*
Bernhard Ulmann Co., Bear Brand
Win Knit, Art. 7116 in
No. 449 Purple, No. 430
Natural, and No. 498 Blue.

Head Scarf and Belt: *stockinette stitch and garter stitch on the bias for the scarf. Coats & Clark's Red Heart Knitting Worsted (100% wool), Art. E. 234 in No. 253 Tangerine and No. 111 Eggshell.*

Head Scarf and Belt

Materials: knitting worsted (4-oz. skein). 1 skein each of 2 colors.

Needles: 1 pair No. 8 or English No. 5

Gauge: scarf: 4 sts = 1 inch; belt: 5 sts = 1 inch

Finished size: scarf: 23 inches at cast-off edges; belt: 82 inches long, 2 inches wide

Pattern: scarf: stockinette stitch, garter stitch edge, yarn over on the bias; belt: garter stitch

DIRECTIONS

Scarf

Cast on 2 sts in first color. Row 1: K 1, yo, k 1. Row 2: K 3. Row 3: K 1, yo, k 1, yo, k 1. Row 4: K 5. Row 5: K 2, yo, k 1, yo, k 2. Row 6: K 7. Row 7: K 3, yo, k 1, yo, k 3. Row 8: K 3, p 3, k 3. Row 9: K 3, yo, k 3, yo, k 3. Row 10: K 3, p 5, k 3. Row 11: K 3, yo, k 5, yo, k 3. Row 12: K 3, p 7, k 3. Continue with first color, inc in this way until you have 19 sts, ending on purl row (row 18). Change to second color and continue inc in this way for 10 rows more (29 sts). Change to first color and continue inc in this way for 8 rows more (37 sts). Change to second color and continue inc in this way for 10 rows more (47 sts). Change to first color and continue inc in this way for 8 rows more (55 sts). Change to second color and continue inc in this way for 10 rows more (65 sts). Change to first color and continue inc in this way for 8 rows more (73 sts). Change to second color and continue inc in this way for 10 rows more (83 sts). Change to first color and continue inc in this way for 8 rows more (91 sts). K 2 rows. Cast off.

To finish: Block. Make a tassel with 12 pieces of each color (24 pieces) 12 inches long (see page 40). Add to the point of the scarf. You can also make braided tie cords to fasten the scarf under your chin (see page 41).

Belt

Cast on 11 sts in second color. K 18 rows. Change to first color. K 18 rows. Repeat each color in order 5 more times. (Make sure it is long enough to go around your waist; knit another two stripes if you have to.) Change to second color. K 18 rows. Cast off.

To finish: For fringe, cut 18 pieces of yarn (9 pieces of each color) 12 inches long. Use 3 pieces of yarn for each unit of fringe (see page 39). Attach 3 units of fringe at each end of belt.

Variations

Each stripe can be a different color. To make a hat from the scarf, fold the two points to the beginning of the scarf and sew the edges together. You can make the belt shorter and wear it as a headband or around your neck.

Slippers

Materials: rug yarn (cotton and rayon, colorfast; 70-yd. skein). 1 skein each of 2 colors.

Needles: 1 pair No. 9 or English No. 4

Gauge: 4 sts = 1 inch (garter stitch)

Finished size: Medium child's size or small adult (for large size, cast on 31 sts and increase all directions by 2 rows each)

Pattern: garter stitch and rib stitch (Row 1: * K 1, p 1, repeat from * across row, to last stitch, k 1. Row 2: * P 1, k 1, repeat from * across row to last stitch, p 1)

DIRECTIONS

Cast on 29 sts with first color. K 20 rows. Change to second color. K 8, p 1, k 11, p 1, k 8. Repeat 10 more times. K rib pattern for 8 rows. Change to first color. Knit rib pattern for 18 rows. *Do not* cast off.

To finish: While stitches are still on the needle, cut 12 inches of yarn from the ball. Thread the yarn into a tapestry needle, pulling the yarn double. To close the toe, slip the stitches off the needle onto the threaded tapestry needle, making sure to keep stitches from being dropped. When all the stitches are transferred to the yarn, pull the yarn ends together and knot them securely. Trim ends to 1 inch and work ends into edges. Sew the slipper together the length of the rib. At the heel, fold the cast-on edge in half and sew edges together. Repeat for the second slipper.

Pompom: Wind yarn lengthwise around a 6-inch ruler 26 times. Tie the yarn tightly on both sides of the ruler at the 3-inch mark. Cut the yarn at both ends of the ruler. Sew the pompom to the slipper at the color change. Clip the ends evenly. Repeat for the second slipper.

Variations

Make slippers in one solid color, to match a robe, or use an ombré yarn.

Slippers: rib stitch and garter stitch. American Thread Co., Aunt Lydia's Heavy Rug Yarn (cotton and rayon, colorfast), Art. 235 in turquoise and pink.

Autumn Scarf

Materials: knitting worsted (twin-pack, 1¾-oz. ball). 4 balls ombré.

Needles: 1 pair No. 8 or English No. 5

Gauge: 4½ sts = 1 inch (check stitch)

Finished size: 44 inches without fringe; 11 inches wide at cast-on edge

Pattern: 4 × 4 rib stitch and check stitch

DIRECTIONS

Cast on 52 sts. (A) (check pattern) Row 1: * K 4, p 4, repeat from * across row, ending k 4. Row 2: * P 4, k 4, repeat from * across row, ending p 4. Repeat rows 1 and 2 once more. Row 5: * P 4, k 4, repeat from * across row, ending p 4. Row 6: * K 4, p 4, repeat from * across row, ending k 4. Repeat rows 5 and 6 once more. Repeat (A) 11 more times. (B) (rib pattern) Row 1: * K 4, p 4, repeat from * across row, ending k 4. Row 2: * P 4, k 4, repeat from * across row, ending p 4. Repeat (B) for 16 inches. Repeat (A) 19 times. Cast off in pattern.

To finish: Cut 84 pieces of yarn 12 inches long for fringe (3 pieces of yarn for each unit of fringe). Attach a unit of fringe at the beginning of each check (see page 39).

Variations

You can use synthetic yarn if you prefer. If you use a lightweight yarn and smaller needles, you can make a finer, dressier scarf. For a change, work garter stitch at the beginning and end instead of check stitch.

Autumn Scarf: rib stitch
and check stitch.
Bernhard Ulmann Co.,
Bear Brand 100% Wool
Knitting Worsted in
No. X06 Ombré (shades
of brown and white).

Tasseled Hat: *stockinette stitch and rib stitch. Bernhard Ulmann Co., Bernhard Ulmann Co., Bucilla Wool and Shetland, Art. 7214 in No. 233 Lime Twist, No. 703 Oxford Gray, and No. 1 White.*

Tasseled Hat

Materials: wool and Shetland mixture (2-oz. ball). 1 ball each of 3 colors.

Needles: 1 pair No. 7 or English No. 4

Gauge: 4½ sts = 1 inch (stockinette stitch)

Finished size: average

Pattern: stockinette stitch and 2 × 2 rib stitch (Row 1: * K 2, p 2, repeat from * across row. Row 2: * P 2, k 2, repeat from * across row)

DIRECTIONS

Leave 8 inches of yarn at the beginning and end of each color change to be used later as part of the fringe. Cast on 100 sts in first color. * Work rib pattern 5 times. Change to second color. Work rib pattern 5 times. Change to third color. Work rib pattern 5 times. Change to first color and repeat from *, only reduce number of rows to 4 for each color. Change to first color. Row 1: * K 4, k 2 tog, repeat from * across row. Row 2: P. Work stockinette stitch for 4 more rows. Change to second color. Repeat rows 1 through 6. Change to third color and repeat rows 1 through 6. Continue dec in this way, alternating colors, ending with p 3 tog. Cast off.

To finish: Sew hat together. Sew the end of the yarn where the color change comes to the beginning end and leave both ends outside. Continue in this way until you have joined all the ends. For fringe, cut 2 pieces of each color 9 inches long. Pull 2 pieces through hat next to the yarn already there and tie with a gathering knot. When the fringe is finished, trim the ends evenly.

Variations

You can, of course, make the hat in one solid color, or you can vary the stripes.

Place Mat

Materials: carpet warp (colorfast; 600-yd. spool). 2 spools make 3 mats. (See directions for spool box, page 14.)

Needles: 1 pair No. 8 or English No. 5

Gauge: 4 sts = 1 inch (seed stitch)

Finished size: 12½ inches by 18½ inches

Pattern: Seed stitch and leaf stitch. Seed: Row A: * K 1, p 1, repeat from * across row, ending p 1. Row B: * P 1, k 1, repeat from * across row, ending k 1. Leaf: Row 1: * Yo, k 3 tog, yo, k 3, repeat from * across row. Rows 2 and 4: P. Row 3: * K 3, yo, k 3 tog, yo, repeat from * across row.

DIRECTIONS

Cast on 74 sts (double strand). Work rows A and B 7 times. Repeat row A. Put markers on after first 10 sts and before last 10 sts. Work seed st for 10 sts, purl to last 10 sts, work last 10 sts in seed st. (The first 10 sts and the last 10 sts are in seed st on every row during the leaf pattern rows and are not included in the general directions.) Work leaf pattern 13 times. Work rows A and B 8 times. Cast off, keeping pattern.

To finish: Block, using medium solution of liquid starch.

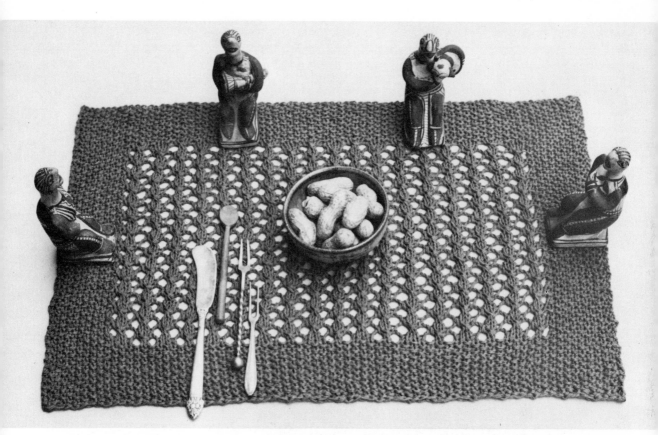

Place Mat: *seed stitch and leaf stitch.*
Dick Blick (Gatesburg, Illinois),
Maysville Carpet Warp (colorfast),
Art. 2050308 in No. 20 Red.

Stretch Bag: *purse stitch.*
Dick Blick (Gatesburg, Illinois),
Macramé Cord, Art. 2026404
or Art. 2022104 in yellow.

Stretch Bag

Materials: macramé cord (60-yd. ball or 250-yd. ball). 3 60-yd. balls. Use 3 larger balls if you want a larger bag. Ten 1-inch curtain rings.

Needles: 1 pair No. 11 (no English size)

Gauge: 4 sts = 1 inch

Finished size: 12 inches by 13 inches

Pattern: purse stitch (all rows: * Yo, p 2 tog, repeat from * across row)

DIRECTIONS

Bag

Measure and cut cord for braid before starting bag. When you are knitting, remember to pull the cord from the center of the ball. Cast on 36 sts. Rows 1 and 2: K. Row 3: K 2, * yo, p 2 tog, repeat from * across row, ending k 2. Repeat row 3 until work measures 24 inches. K 2 rows. Cast off.

Braid

Cut 12 pieces of cord 50 inches long to make 2 pieces of braid. Use each piece double, or 6 pieces for each 3-strand braid (see page 41). Leave 6 inches of cord unbraided at beginning and end.

To finish: Fold in half. Pin sides together and sew loosely, leaving 3 inches open on each side at the top. Sew 5 rings across the top on both sides (1 at each end, 3 in the middle). Insert braid through 10 rings, ending each braid at opposite ends. Make overhand knots of 4 strands of cord each, leaving a tassel at the end.

Christmas Bag

Materials: knitting worsted (either 100% wool or 4-ply synthetic). 3½ oz. green and 2 oz. white. Ten bells, 2 brass rings, 2 pieces red felt (8 inches by 12 inches), a piece of red yarn for finishing.

Needles: 1 pair No. 9 or English No. 4

Gauge: 4½ sts = 1 inch (stockinette stitch)

Finished size: 14 inches by 16 inches before folding

Pattern: Lace stitch (on 7 stitches) and stockinette stitch. Lace: Row 1: K 1, yo, k 2 tog, k 3, yo, k 1 (8 sts). Row 2 and all even number rows through 10: K. Row 3: K 1, yo, k 2 tog, k 4, yo, k 1 (9 sts). Row 5: K 1, yo, k 2 tog, k 5, yo, k 1 (10 sts). Row 7: K 1, yo, k 2 tog, k 6, yo, k 1 (11 sts). Row 9: Cast off 4 sts, k 6 (7 sts). (Helpful hint: When you knit the first row, put a marker on your needle after the 7th st and before the last 2 sts.)

DIRECTIONS

Bag
Cast on 54 sts in green. * Row 1: Work row 1 of lace pattern (put on 1st marker), k across row to last 2 sts (put on 2nd marker), k 2. Row 2: K 2, p across row to marker, k remaining sts. Continue lace pattern rows 3 through 10, keeping remainder of sts in stockinette stitch, except for 2 sts at other edge, which are in garter. Repeat from * 9 more times. Cast off.

Christmas Bag: lace stitch and stockinette stitch. Knitting worsted in Christmas green, white, and red.

Lace Skirt

Cast on 8 sts in white. Work lace pattern 10 times, ending each odd number row k 2. Cast off.

Lace for Top of Bag

Cast on 12 sts in white. Knit first 7 sts in lace pattern, put on marker. After marker, in all odd number rows, yo, k 2 tog, k 3. Even number rows: K. (These 5 sts are to give extra width to the lace and to give space for weaving in the red yarn when finishing the bag.) Work pattern 10 times. Cast off.

To finish: Block each piece carefully. Sew beginning and end together to make the side seam. Sew the bag together where the lace pattern begins to make the bottom of the bag. Sew the pieces of felt together on 3 sides, leaving a ½-inch hem on each side. Put the lining in the bag, and turn the extra lining at the top so that it fits just below the 2-stitch border. Stitch the lining to the bag. Fit the wide piece of lace around the top of the bag, just below the 2-stitch border. Stitch it to the bag with red yarn. Attach a bell to each point of lace. Join the second piece of lace (lace skirt) under the green lace at the bottom of the bag, using a double strand of red yarn. Weave the yarn through the holes in the lace, pulling the piece in slightly at the bottom. Sew one brass ring to the top at the seam line and the other opposite it.

Doll

Materials: Orlon acrylic rug yarn (4-oz. skein). 2 skeins each of 2 colors, and 1 skein in third color. Two 1¼-inch brass rings, two ¾-inch movable eye buttons, one 1¼-inch loop buckle for the nose, one 1½-inch loop buckle for the mouth, and 1 pound kapok for stuffing.

Needles: 1 No. 10 circular (29 inches long) and extra needle to hold stitches

Gauge: 3 sts = 1 inch (stockinette)

Finished size: 20½ inches head to foot

Pattern: 2 × 2 rib stitch, stockinette stitch, and rice stitch (Row 1: K. Row 2: K 1, p 1 across row)

DIRECTIONS

Legs (front)

Cast on 18 sts in first color. Row 1: * K 2, p 2, repeat from * across row, ending k 2. Row 2: * P 2, k 2, repeat from * across row, ending p 2. Repeat rows 1 and 2, 13 more times. Repeat rows 1 and 2 twice more (4 rows), inc 1 st at the beginning and end of each row (26 sts). Do not cast off. Cut off yarn, leaving 16 inches. Transfer leg to extra needle. Repeat to make second leg. Leave second leg on needle.

Body (front)

Put first leg back on circular needle with the 16 inches of loose yarn in the middle, between the two legs. Work row 1, inc 1 st at the end of first leg and 1 st at the beginning of second leg (this gives 2 p sts in the middle; total 54 sts). Continue across row. Repeat rows 1 and 2 twice more. Work 4 rows in rice pattern. Change to second color. Continue in rice pattern for 38 rows. K 1 row, dec 1 st at the beginning of the row (sl 1, k 1, psso), and k 2 tog at end. Begin stockinette st. Continue dec

at beginning and end of every knit row until 40 sts remain. P one row. Continue dec at the beginning and end of every row until you have 14 sts. Cast off, leaving 24 inches of yarn for sewing piece together.

Legs (back)
Work exactly the same as the front.

Body (back)
Join in legs as for front, and work as for front. Instead of changing to stockinette stitch, however, at the beginning of the dec, continue to work in rice stitch until casting off.

Arms
Cast on 20 sts in first color. Work rib st for 28 rows. K 1 row, inc 1 st at the beginning and end of the row (22 sts). Work stockinette st for 6 rows, inc 1 st at the beginning and end of the 6th row (24 sts). Work 9 rows in stockinette st, inc 1 st at the beginning and end of the 9th row (26 sts). Work stockinette st for 5 more rows, inc 1 st at the beginning and end of the 5th row (28 sts). Work stockinette st for 5 more rows. K 1 row, cast off 3 sts at beginning of row. P 1 row, cast off 3 sts at the beginning of row. Continue dec 1 st at the beginning and end of every row to 8 sts. P 1 row. Cast off. Repeat for second arm.

To finish: Pin the pieces together with the right sides of the fabric on the outside.

Doll: 2 x 2 rib stitch, stockinette stitch, and rice stitch. Woolworth Woolco, Craft and Rug Yarn, 100% Dupont Orlon Acrylic, Art. 107 in No. 253 Tangerine, No. 111 Eggshell, and No. 764 Deep Purple.

Legs: Sew the sides together. Fill with kapok. Sew across the tops of the legs, where the color changes, to allow the legs to fold.

Body: Sew one side and across the top. Fill with kapok evenly. Sew other side.

Arms: Sew the sides of the arms together. Pin the top of the arm to the body of the doll where the stitch pattern changes from rice stitch to stockinette stitch. Pin half to the front and half to the back across the top. Pin the sides straight down in line with the seam of the body. Sew carefully to the doll. Fill arms with kapok and sew the ends.

Hair: Use third color yarn for hair (see fringe on page 39). There are 5 units of fringe on each side. For each unit of fringe cut 6 pieces of yarn 12 inches long. Attach fringe as described on page 40. Leave 3 inches of space in the middle.

Eyes: For lashes, knot five 6-inch-long pieces of yarn to a brass ring for each eye. Sew rings on. Sew on an eye button in the center of each ring.

Nose: Sew on smaller loop buckle at the top only (on the straight edge) with first color yarn.

Mouth: Follow *Nose* directions, using the larger loop buckle.

Variation

You can be as creative as you like with this project—the legs can be longer, the arms shorter, the hair done in braids. You can add gloves and shoes, and if you make the body longer, you can add a belt. Let your imagination run wild.

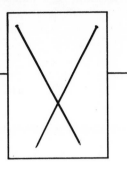

SUGGESTED READING

Abbey, Barbara. *The Complete Book of Knitting*. New York: Viking Press, 1971.

Fougner, Dave. *The Manly Art of Knitting*. Santa Rosa, Calif.: Threshold, 1972.

Meyer, Carolyn. *Yarn: The Things It Makes and How to Make Them*. New York: Harcourt Brace Jovanovich, 1972.

Phillips, Mary Walker. *Creative Knitting*. New York: Van Nostrand Reinhold, 1971.

————. *Step-by-Step Knitting*. New York: Golden Press, 1967.

————. *Step-by-Step Macramé*. New York: Golden Press, 1970 (for additional fringe ideas).

Thomas, Mary. *Mary Thomas's Knitting Book*. New York: Dover, 1972.
————. *Mary Thomas's Pattern Book*. New York: Dover, 1972.

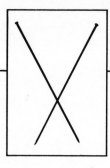

INDEX

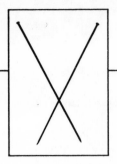

ABOUT THE AUTHOR

Mary Walker Phillips was the first person to explore knitting as an independent art form, giving new meaning to an ancient folk craft. Her innovative knitting, macramé, and textile designs have been widely exhibited, and her work is represented in the permanent collections of the Museum of Modern Art, the Smithsonian Institution, the Museum of Contemporary Crafts, and "Objects: U.S.A.," and in private collections.

After majoring in art at Fresno State College in California, Miss Phillips received bachelor's and master's degrees of Fine Arts in Experimental Textiles at the Cranbrook Academy of Art in Michigan. She lives in New York City when she isn't traveling all over the country, conducting workshops in contemporary knitting and macramé; she also participates in national and international craft groups and conferences. Besides writing numerous magazine articles, she is the author of *Step-by-Step Knitting*, *Step-by-Step Macramé*, and *Creative Knitting*; she is a contributing author to *Encyclopedia of Crafts*.